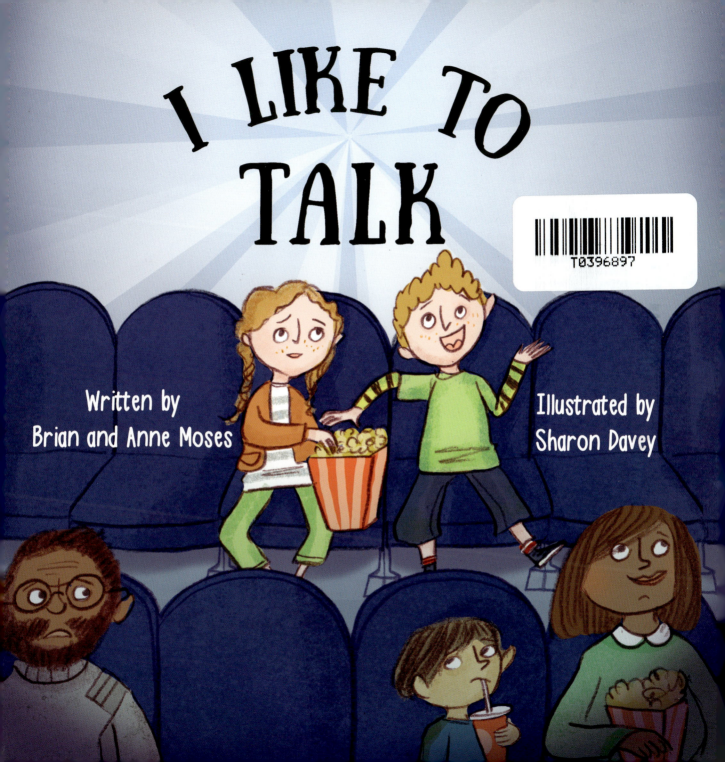

First published in Great Britain in 2022 by The Watts Publishing Group
Copyright © The Watts Publishing Group, 2022
First published in Great Britain in 2022 by The Watts Publishing Group
Copyright © The Watts Publishing Group, 2022

Author: Brian and Anne Moses
Series Editor: Melanie Palmer
Series Design: Lisa Peacock
Literacy Consultant: Kate Ruttle
Editorial director: Kathy Middleton
Illustrator: Sharon Davey
Editor: Janine Deschenes
Proofreader: Petrice Custance
Production technician: Margaret Salter
Print coordinator: Katherine Berti

Library and Archives Canada Cataloguing in Publication
Available at the Library of Congress Canada

Library of Congress Cataloging-in-Publication Data
Available at the Library of Congress

Crabtree Publishing Company
www.crabtreebooks.com   1-800-387-7650

Published by Crabtree Publishing Company in 2022.

All rights reserved. No part of this publication may be reproduced, stored in a retrieval system or be transmitted in any form or by any means, electronic, mechanical, photocopying, recording, or otherwise, without the prior written permission of Crabtree Publishing Company. In Canada: We acknowledge the financial support of the Government of Canada through the Canada Book Fund for our publishing activities.

Printed in the U.S.A./012022/CG20210915

Published in Canada
Crabtree Publishing
616 Welland Ave.
St. Catharines, Ontario
L2M 5V6

Published in the United States
Crabtree Publishing
347 Fifth Ave
Suite 1402-145
New York, NY 10016

I LIKE TO TALK

Written by
Brian and Anne Moses

Illustrated by
Sharon Davey

CRABTREE
PUBLISHING COMPANY
WWW.CRABTREEBOOKS.COM

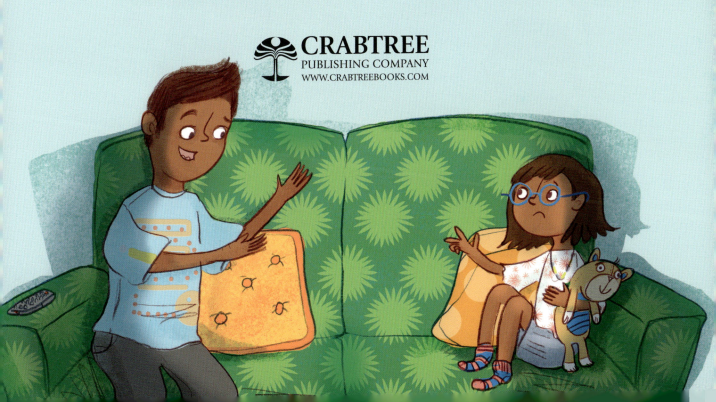

Levi's twin sister thinks that Levi talks too much sometimes. She wishes he would stay quiet at the movies. Too much talking during a movie is distracting!

During dinner, Levi finds a picture of the spaceship that he saw in the movie. He talks excitedly about how it flies.

Levi's mom lets him finish. Then, she asks Levi's sister how she enjoyed the movie.

Hannah and her dad are watching a TV show about four children who got trapped in a cave. Hannah feels afraid for the children. She tells her dad that she feels scared and upset.

Hannah's dad gives her a hug. He explains that the children will be rescued soon. Hannah is glad she told her dad how she felt. She feels much better.

On their way home from the grocery store, William and Danny see a girl fall off her bike. She's crying and in a lot of pain. They think she hurt her leg.

The school nurse looks at her knee. She asks Wang Li where it hurts. Wang Li points to the spot. She explains that it throbs and stings.

Levi and William are making a model of a castle. They take turns to share their ideas.

At school, a children's author is visiting. She is telling everyone about the way she writes her books.

The author invites the children to write a short story with her. It will be about a special dog. The children brainstorm ideas about the dog.

Sometimes, the things we say hurt other people's feelings.

Hannah feels like crying when two classmates say unkind things about her new haircut.

Wang Li feels upset when a friend jokes about her soccer uniform. Her mom and dad were not able to wash her uniform before practice. She borrowed some clothes instead.

Levi is upset because William broke the remote control for his toy car. He feels like yelling. But he knows that yelling at William is hurtful.

Sometimes Wang Li's little brother feels very shy and does not want to speak to strangers. Wang Li helps. She speaks for him.

The children are performing in a school play. Everyone feels nervous! The teacher reminds them to speak loud and clear so the audience can hear them.

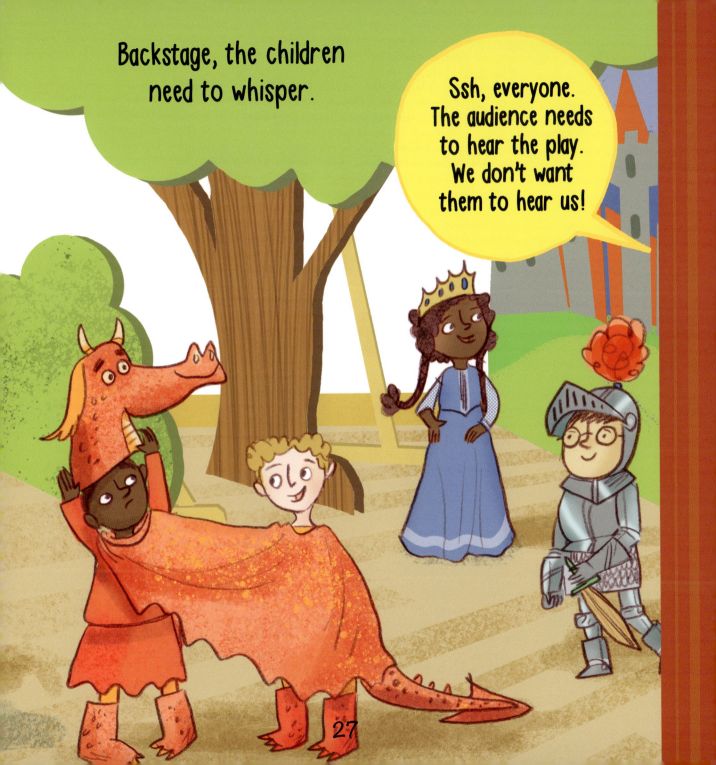

To help keep in touch with friends and family all over the world, we can talk online or on the phone.

Wang Li video chats with her aunt and uncle in China.

Hannah and her family keep in contact with some of their family in India.

Talking brings everyone closer together.

NOTES FOR CAREGIVERS AND EDUCATORS

This book shows children that talking is an important form of communication. From sharing ideas and expressing feelings to brainstorming and solving problems, children will be encouraged to improve their verbal communication skills. Here are some ideas for how to get the most from this book.

Pages 4-5
Ask children to think about all the different people they might talk to in a school day, such as teachers, office staff, friends, crossing guards, etc. Can they think of things they might say to each of these people?

Pages 6-7 and 8-9
Talk about a movie or TV show. Which character is their favorite? What parts did children find funny? What parts made them feel upset, scared, or worried?

Pages 10-11
Reread the grocery store scenario. Ask children how William and Danny came to an agreement. Help them understand that the brothers talked with each other to make a compromise. Talk to children about a time that they compromised. What was it like? How did talking help them reach an agreement?

Pages 12-13 and 14-15
Talk through what to do when someone needs help. Who should children talk to? Go through how to make a phone call to 911 and when it is appropriate to do so. If a child is hurt, what do they need to tell others? Why was it helpful that Wang Li told the nurse where she was hurt?

Pages 16-17
If children have been to a museum or special exhibition, ask them what they can remember about it. What was their favorite part of the visit? Was there a model or object there that impressed them?

Pages 18-19
Read books together, particularly ones where children can join in on repeating choruses. Try leaving out a word and asking children to guess what it is. Encourage children to brainstorm ideas for stories and rhymes. Play around with words to create poems and stories.

Pages 20-21 and 22-23
Reread the scenarios on these pages. Ask children how they might feel in Wang Li, Hannah, Levi, or William's shoes. Why is it important to consider how our words impact others?

Pages 24-25
Ask children how they might show someone they are happy, angry, or sad without using words. Play a game of charades with cards that have emotions on them. Talk about how body language affects the meaning of the words we speak.

Pages 26-27
Have children partipate in show-and-tell. Give each child a minute to share a favorite toy, book, keepsake, etc. Remind them to speak clearly.

Pages 28-29
Play a game of telephone. Have children sit in a circle. Whisper a message in the first child's ear. Each child whispers the message to the person next to them, until everyone has heard the message. The last child reveals what they heard. Talk about how the final message compared to the initial one.

31

BOOKS TO SHARE

I Spy with My Little Eye series
by Amy Culliford, illustrated by Srimalie Bassani (Crabtree Publishing, 2022)

Samuel Scaredosaurus (Dinosaurs Have Feelings, Too)
by Brian Moses, illustrated by Mike Gordon (B.E.S. Publishing, 2014)

There's an Alien in Your Book
by Tom Fletcher, illustrated by Greg Abbott (Random House Books for Young Readers, 2021)

The Worrysaurus
by Rachel Bright, illustrated by Chris Chatterton (Orchard Books, 2020)

We're Going on a Bear Hunt
by Michael Rosen, illustrated by Helen Oxenbury (Scholastic, 2020)